MW01044600

COTTAGE CHARM

Cozy Quilts and Cross Stitch Projects

By Dawn Heese

COTTAGE CHARM

Cozy Quilts and Cross Stitch Projects

By Dawn Heese

Editor: Kimber Mitchell
Designer: Bob Deck
Photography: Aaron T. Leimkuehler
Illustration: Lon Eric Craven
Technical Editor: Kathe Dougherty
Production assistance: Jo Ann Groves

Published by:
Kansas City Star Books
1729 Grand Blvd.
Kansas City, Missouri, USA 64108

All rights reserved
Copyright © 2010 Kansas City Star Co.
No part of this book may be reproduced, stored
in a retrieval system, or transmitted in any
form or by any means, electronic, mechanical,
photocopying, recording or otherwise, without
prior consent of the publisher.

First edition, first printing
ISBN: 978-1-935362-56-2

Library of Congress Control
Number: 2010930359

Printed in the United States of America
By Walsworth Publishing Co., Marceline, MO

To order copies, call StarInfo at
(816) 234-4636 and say "Books."

KANSAS CITY STAR
Quilts
Continuing the Tradition

PickleDish.com
The Quilter's Home Page

About the Author

Dawn Heese is a third-generation quilter and an avid cross stitcher. Inspired by a quilt pattern in a magazine, she bought her first rotary cutter and mat in 1999 and hasn't stopped quilting since. She particularly enjoys needleturn appliqué and hand quilting. Her love of traditional patterns stems from fond childhood memories of being surrounded by quilts.

Dawn lives in Columbia, Missouri, where she also works as a hairstylist. She is a member of the Boonslick Trail Quilters Guild as well as an appliqué group and quilt study group. Dawn teaches at her local quilt shops as well as quilt guilds. This is her second book with Kansas City Star Quilts. Her first book was *Geese in the Rose Garden.* Follow Dawn's quilting adventures and get free quilt patterns at her blog, dawnheesequilts.blogspot.com.

CONTENTS

Several words come to mind when I think of cottage style. Cozy, casual, and comforting are at the top of that list, but I also think of the word "handmade". In these busy times, our homes are our refuge and I think we all seek to create an environment that is soothing to the soul. Handmade creations such as quilts and cross stitch projects can enhance that inviting ambience. One of the things I love about cottage style is that it often mixes old and new to create the unexpected. It's like pairing your grandma's silver with new funky dinnerware.

A blend of old and new, the designs featured in this book are a fresh take on vintage patterns. Two of the quilts were inspired by quilt designs that my great grandmother used in the 1940s. I incorporated elements from her quilts into my designs while taking them in a new direction. Vermillion, for example, combines the beauty of appliquéd tulips with two different pieced blocks. Gossamer features butterflies in flight, surrounded by a narrow scalloped border. The classic Rose of Sharon block plays a starring role in the In My Garden quilt, but I gave the overall look a fresh twist by carrying the vines of those blocks out to the seam allowances and introducing an element of the unexpected— carrots and bunnies.

To complement the quilts, I designed three quick cross stitch projects. As much as I love appliqué, it is nice to be able to sit and quickly stitch projects like these. They make great decorative accents for your home as well as wonderful handmade gifts for friends and family. For some decorating inspiration, be sure to check out all the beautiful photography in this book. Whether you love cross stitch or quilting, I hope you'll find a project within these pages to make your home even more inviting.

Dawn

DEDICATION

This book is dedicated to the many wonderful, creative women in my family.

ACKNOWLEDGEMENTS

You've heard the phrase "It takes a village" as it applies to raising a child. Well, it also rings particularly true when it comes to publishing a book. The finished product is so much more than just my initial idea and the designs it inspires. There are many talented people who worked hard to make this book happen. I can honestly say that I love the team at Kansas City Star Quilts and couldn't ask for any better.

When expressing my thanks, I always have to start with Doug Weaver and Diane McLendon. They took a chance on an unknown designer and are still behind me. I wouldn't be writing this book without them.

A heartfelt thank you also goes to Kimber Mitchell, the world's best editor, friend, and fellow quilter.

My thanks also to:
Bob Deck for his design work on this book as well as my previous book, *Geese in the Rose Garden*.

Aaron T. Leimkuehler for his always-gorgeous photography.

Kathe Dougherty for double checking my quilting math, Lon Eric Craven for his wonderful artwork, and Jo Ann Groves for fine-tuning the photos.

And many, many thanks to Debbie Dusenberry at the Curious Sofa in Prairie Village, Kansas. Deb's gorgeous store provided the backdrop and "eye candy" for the book. I am forever grateful for the opportunity to do the shoot there. If you haven't been to the Curious Sofa, I suggest you go right away or at least check it out at www.curioussofa.com. And try not to drool!

Christy Gray for the beautiful quilting on the Vermillion and Gossamer quilts.

Weeks Dye Works for providing all the floss used in the cross stitch projects.

Moda Fabrics for the fat quarter bundle used in the Gossamer quilt.

And once again, many thanks to my family for being so tolerant of the time I spent working on the book and for surviving my many meltdowns as the deadlines approached.

There are many ways to appliqué. My way is not the "right way", just the method that works best for me. I love to appliqué by hand rather than machine, but I don't like to spend my time on prep work. I prefer to get right to the stitching! Since I carry my appliqué with me practically everywhere I go, my method requires very few supplies so I don't have to tote a ton of them along. Here are the basics for my appliqué technique.

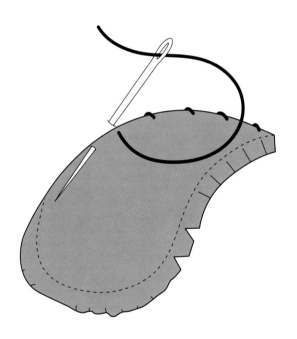

I. Trace the template shapes on the dull side of a piece of freezer paper. Do not add a seam allowance to the templates. Cut out on the drawn line. The freezer paper will adhere to the fabric many times. If you need four of the same leaf, for example, you need only cut one paper template and reuse it.

2. When I cut my background fabric squares to size, I seal their edges with Fray Check to prevent raveling and distortion.

3. Fold your background fabric square in half vertically and horizontally, finger pressing the folds. Then fold on both diagonals and finger press. These fold lines will serve as a guide for placing the appliqué shapes on the background fabric.

4. Iron the paper templates, shiny side down, to the right side of the fabric. Using a chalk pencil (I prefer Generals brand as they mark easily), trace around the template. Make sure the line is clearly visible as this will be your turn line. Add an ⅛"- ¼" seam allowance around the template, then cut it out.

5. Pin or baste the appliqué shape in place on the background fabric square. I like Clover appliqué pins as they have a thick shaft that keeps them from backing out of the piece. Their oval heads are also less likely to snag your thread.

6. Sew the appliqué shapes in the order that they are layered, starting with the bottom pieces. Use the tip of your needle or a toothpick to turn under your seam allowance.

7. When appliquéing, I recommend using YLI 100-weight silk thread in a neutral shade because it sinks into the fabric and practically disappears. Using a neutral color also means you won't have to worry about matching all the pieces with coordinating thread colors.

The cross stitch projects and the Gossamer quilt featured in this book use a variety of hand stitches—a counted cross stitch, French knot, backstitch, and lazy daisy stitch. To learn how to create them, see the following diagrams.

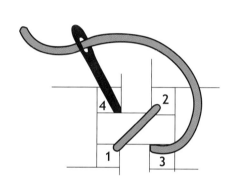

Counted Cross Stitch

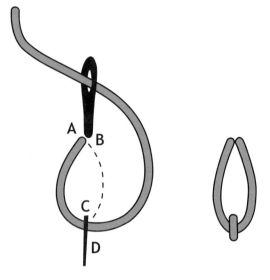

Lazy Daisy Stitch

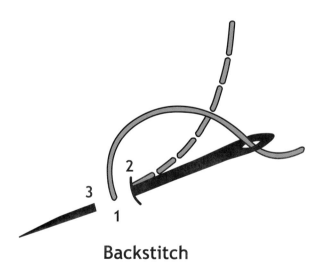

Backstitch

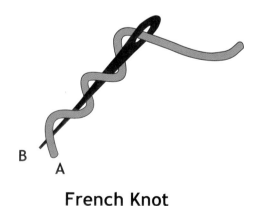

French Knot

Bias binding is used for curved borders such as the scalloped ones featured in the Gossamer and In My Garden quilts. This is because bias strips have a natural stretch to them that allows you to easily follow the curves of the quilt. Here is a fast and easy method for cutting them.

1. Fold your fabric in half diagonally to form a 45-degree angle.

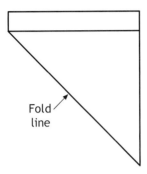

2. Fold a second time by bringing the top left corner down to the bottom right corner, creating a second 45-degree angle. Smooth the fabric.

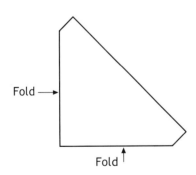

3. Cut off the fold on the left side of the triangle.

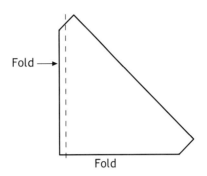

4. Cut your strips whatever width you prefer. Typically, I cut either a 2" or a 2 ¼" strip for a durable double-fold binding.

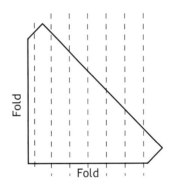

5. Join the strips on the diagonal.

11

VERMILLION

Finished size: 64" x 64"
Finished appliqué block: 13 ½"
Finished pieced block: 9"
Hand appliquéd and machine pieced by Dawn Heese
Machine quilted by Christy Gray/Katydid Design Studio

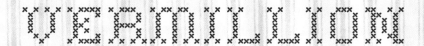

At first glance, this appears to be a two-color quilt, but it actually uses 12 different reds and 2 different cream backgrounds. The result is a two-color look that adds visual interest by using various shades of the same color. The appliqué blocks were redrafted from a quilt made for my mother by her grandmother. The original version was created with solid-color fabrics, and its blocks were smaller and combined with setting squares. For my version, I thought the appliqué made a striking focal point in the center of the quilt, surrounded by pieced blocks. Polka dot fabric enlivens the tulip centers as well as the narrow border, while the combination of the chain and star blocks adds a sense of movement throughout the rest of the quilt.

Fabric Requirements

Appliqué and pieced blocks:
- 3 ¾ yards total of two different cream prints for block backgrounds

Pieced blocks:
- 2 ⅜ yards total of 11 different red prints for stars and chains

Appliqué blocks:
- ¾ yard of 12th red print for tulip sides and tulip block diamonds
- Fat quarter green print for stems
- Scraps or ⅛ yard gold print for circular centers
- Tulip center yardage listed below

Tulip centers and border:
- ½ yard red dot

Backing:
- 2 yards 108"-wide backing fabric

Binding:
- ½ yard red print

TIP

I use Mary Ellen's Best Press to prepare my fabric for appliqué. It removes the most stubborn wrinkles and gives the fabric body.

Cutting Instructions

For tulip blocks, cut:
- 4—14" squares from two different cream prints.
- Appliqué templates on page 21.
- 18" of ½" bias strips from green print per block, using a ½" bias tape maker.

For star blocks, cut:
- 80—2 ¾" squares from two different cream prints for block backgrounds.
- 80—3 ⅛" squares from two different cream prints for block backgrounds.
- 20—5" squares from assorted red prints for stars.
- 80—3 ⅛" squares from assorted red prints for stars.

For chain blocks, cut:
- 20—2" x 16" strips from two different cream prints for block backgrounds.
- 80—3 ½" squares from two different cream prints for block backgrounds.
- 20—2" x 16" strips from assorted red prints for chains.
- 20—3 ½" squares from assorted red prints for chains.

For border, cut:
- 7—1" strips the width of fabric from red polka dot. Then piece these strips to make 2—1" x 63 ½" strips and 2—1" x 64 ½" strips.

For binding, cut red print. Bias binding is not necessary for this project.

Sewing Instructions

TULIP BLOCK

After pinning the templates in place to the first block, it is a good idea to make an appliqué overlay from clear vinyl. This will help to ensure a uniform look when arranging the shapes for the other blocks. Referring to your appliqué overlay for placement, appliqué shapes to the cream print background fabric. Repeat to appliqué a total of 4 blocks.

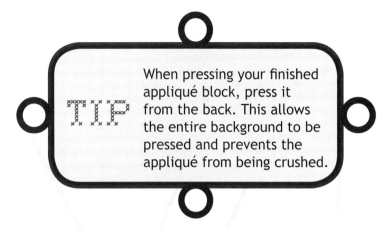

TIP

When pressing your finished appliqué block, press it from the back. This allows the entire background to be pressed and prevents the appliqué from being crushed.

STAR BLOCK

1. With a ruler and pencil, mark a diagonal line from corner to corner on the wrong side of 80—3 ⅛" cream print squares.

2. Right sides together, layer each marked cream square with a 3 ⅛" red print square. Sew a ¼" seam on both sides of the drawn line. Repeat for all 80 pairs of squares.

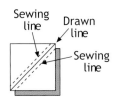

3. Cut on the drawn line to make two half-square triangle units. Make a total of 160 of these units.

4. Press units open. These units will make the star points.

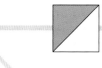

5. Sew 2 of the units created in Step 4 to create the star points. Repeat to create a total of 4 of these units per block.

  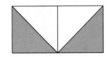

6. Referring to the first and third rows in the diagram below, sew 2—2 ¾" cream print squares to opposite sides of a star point unit created in Step 5. Repeat for the third row.

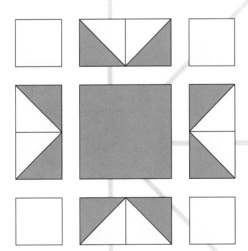

7. Referring to the middle row in the previous diagram, sew two star point units created in Step 5 to opposite sides of a 5" red print square to create the middle row.

8. Join the three rows created in Steps 6 and 7 to create the finished block. Repeat to make a total of 20—9" finished star blocks.

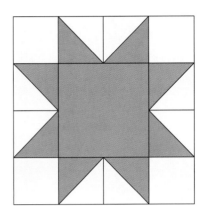

CHAIN BLOCK

1. Right sides together, layer one 2" x 16" cream print strip with one 2" x 16" red print strip. Sew strips together to create a strip set. Press seam toward the red strip. Repeat to make a total of 20 strip sets.

2. Cut the strip sets into 160—2" x 3 ½" units.

3. Join two of the units created in Step 2 to create a 3 ½" four-patch unit. Create a total of 80 of these units.

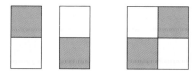

4. Referring to the next diagram, sew two 3 ½" four-patch units to opposite sides of a 3 ½" cream print square. Repeat to make a second row per block.

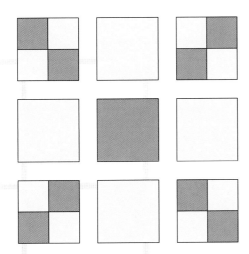

5. Referring to the middle row in the previous diagram, sew 2—3 ½" cream print squares to opposite sides of a 3 ½" red print square. Make one of these rows per block.

6. Join the three rows created in Steps 4 and 5 to create 20—9" finished chain blocks.

Assembling the Quilt Center

1. Referring to the assembly diagram on page 20, sew the 4 appliquéd tulip blocks together, 2 blocks per row.

2. Referring to the assembly diagram on page 20, join 3 chain blocks and 3 star blocks to create the units to the left and right of the appliquéd tulip center.

3. Starting with a star block, sew 4 star blocks alternating with 3 chain blocks. Repeat to make a second row.

4. Starting with a chain block, sew 4 chain blocks alternating with 3 star blocks. Repeat to make a second row.

5. Referring to the assembly diagram on page 20, piece together one row created in Step 3 with one row created in Step 4. Repeat to make a second 2-row unit.

6. Referring to the assembly diagram on page 20, join the 2 units created in Step 2 to the quilt center.

7. Referring to the assembly diagram on page 20 for placement, sew together the three units.

Finishing the Quilt

1. Sew 2—1" x 63 ½" red polka dot strips to each side of the quilt center. Press seams toward the border.

2. Sew 2—1" x 64 ½" red polka dot strips to the top and bottom of the quilt center. Press seams toward the border. This completes the quilt top.

3. Sandwich the quilt top, back, and batting. Baste, quilt, and bind.

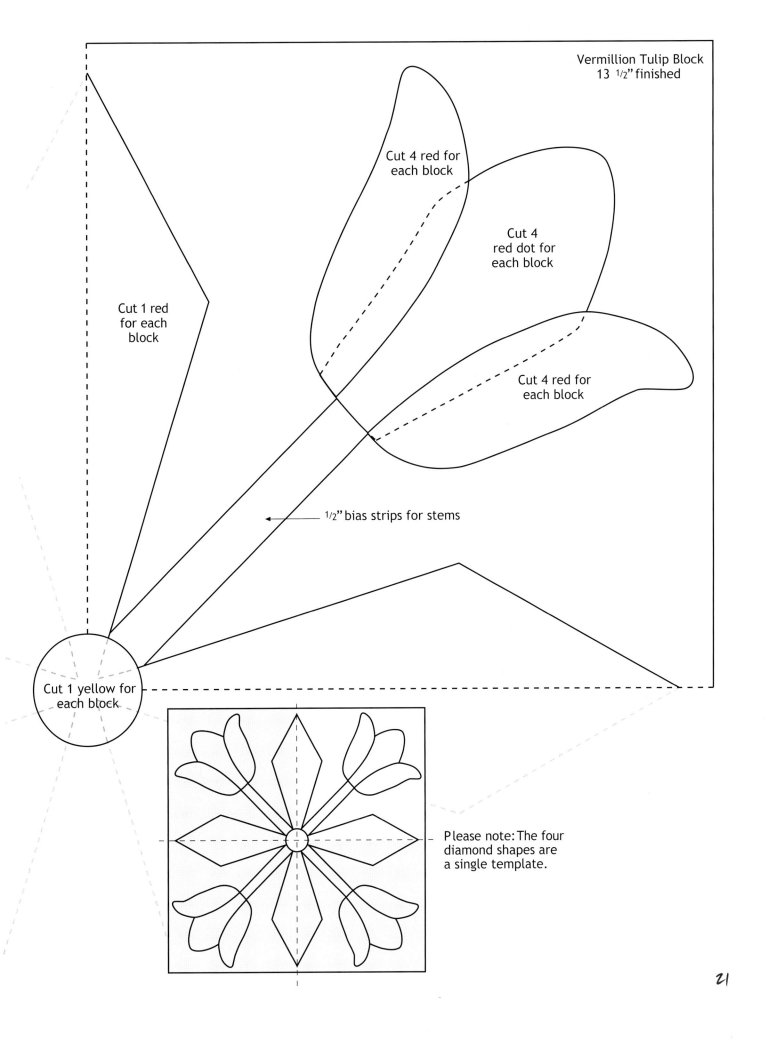

Vermillion Tulip Block
13 ½" finished

Cut 4 red for
each block

Cut 4
red dot for
each block

Cut 4 red for
each block

Cut 1 red
for each
block

½" bias strips for stems

Cut 1 yellow for
each block

Please note: The four
diamond shapes are
a single template.

21

FRESH CUT TULIPS

Fresh Cut Tulips

Finished size: 2.36" x 13.86"
Stitched by Dawn Heese

This garden-fresh greeting comes together quickly and makes a charming companion accent for the Vermillion quilt. It is stitched with 2 strands of floss over 2 threads.

Material Requirements

- 28-count evenweave
- Weeks Dye Works embroidery floss: Moss (2201), Celadon (1261), Liberty (2269), Louisiana Hot Sauce (2266a), and Caper (1266)
- Frame with a 5" x 16" opening

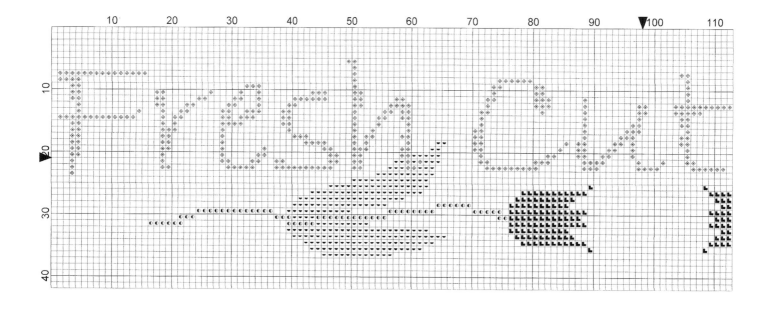

Legend:
◑ WDW-2201
▼ WDW-1261
◣ WDW-2269
◪ WDW-2266a
◈ WDW-1266

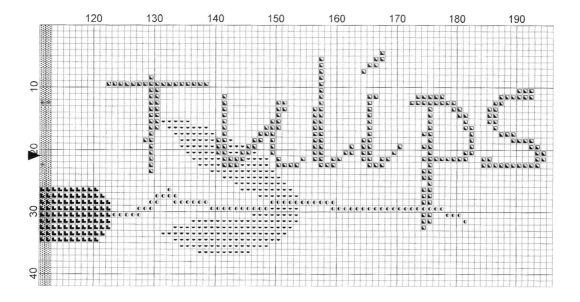

Legend:
◑ WDW-2201
⊖ WDW-1261
◧ WDW-2269
◲ WDW-2266a
◈ WDW-1266

Finished size: 74" x 74"
Finished block size: 18"
Hand appliquéd and hand quilted by Dawn Heese

Bunnies are tucked amid rambling blooms in this fanciful quilt. For the flowering blocks, I chose the classic Rose of Sharon design—with a fun twist. By using larger, more casual blooms and extending the wavy vines right into the seams between blocks, it makes each block appear to flow into the next. Carrots add an unexpected, whimsical element to the central block.

Fabric Requirements

Block backgrounds and outer border:
- 5 yards ticking stripe

Blocks:
- 4 fat quarters pink print for flowers
- 4 fat quarters green print for leaves and stems
- 2 fat quarters blue print for flowers
- One fat quarter orange print for carrots and flower centers
- ¾ yard brown print for bunnies and centers of big flowers

Inner border and binding:
- 1 ¼ yard tangerine print

Backing:
2 ½ yards 108"-wide backing fabric

Cutting Instructions

For carrot block, cut:
- 1—18 ½" square from ticking stripe. Then apply Fray Check around the block edges.
- 24" of ¼" bias strip for stems from green print, using a ¼" bias tape maker.
- Appliqué templates on page 43.

For bloom blocks, cut:
- 4—18 ½" squares from ticking stripe. Then apply Fray Check around the block edges.
- 58" of ¼" bias strip for stems from green print per block, using a ¼" bias tape maker.
- Appliqué templates on page 41.

For bunny blocks, cut:
- 4—18 ½" squares from ticking stripe. Then apply Fray Check around the block edges.
- 21" of ¼" bias strip for stems per block from green print, using a ¼" bias tape maker.
- Appliqué templates on pages 37-39. **Note that you will need to reverse 2 of the 4 bunnies.**

For the inner border, cut:
- 6—2 ½" strips the width of fabric from tangerine print. Then piece these strips to make:
  - 2—2 ½" x 54 ½" strips and
  - 2—2 ½" x 58 ½" strips.
    Be sure to cut the inner border strips BEFORE cutting the bias binding.

For the outer border, cut:
- 8—8 ½" strips the width of fabric from ticking stripe. Then piece these strips to create:
  - 4—8 ½" x 81" strips.
- Scallop template on page 44 from freezer paper.

To create the bias binding, see page 11.

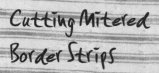

Cutting Mitered Border Strips

To create a mitered border, you first need to figure the length of border strips that you will need. For this quilt, I have already done the math for you (see figures below), but keep this formula handy when creating mitered borders for future quilts:

Miter (3") + border width (8") + quilt center length (58.5") + border width (8") + miter (3") + seam allowance ($^1/_2$") = length of border strips

Sewing Instructions

CARROT BLOCK

Referring to the placement guide on page 42,
appliqué shapes to the background fabric.

BLOOM BLOCK

Referring to the placement guide on page 40,
appliqué the shapes to the background fabric.
Make a total of 4 blocks.

BUNNY BLOCK

Referring to the placement guide on page 36, appliqué shapes to the background fabric. Make a total of 4 blocks. **Note that you will need to reverse 2 of the 4 blocks.**

TIP

After pinning the templates in place to the first block, it is a good idea to make an appliqué overlay from clear vinyl. This will help to ensure a uniform look when arranging the shapes for the other blocks.

Assembling the Quilt Center

1. Referring to the assembly diagram below, lay out blocks in three rows.

2. Sew the blocks into three rows.

3. Sew the three rows together.

INNER BORDER

1. Sew 2—2 ½" x 54 ½" tangerine print strips to the sides of the quilt center.

2. Sew 2—2 ½" x 58 ½" tangerine print strips to the top and bottom of the quilt center.

OUTER BORDER

I used a mitered border, which works great when working with a directional fabric such as the ticking stripe.

1. Find and mark the center of each 8 ½" x 81" ticking stripe border strip. To do this, first match the center of the border strip to the center of one side of the quilt.

2. Right sides together, pin the border strip in place and sew it to the quilt center. When sewing each border strip to the quilt, be sure to start and stop stitching ¼" from the edge of the corners. You will have overhang to make your miter on each side. You can add all four border strips to the quilt center, then miter, or make your miters as you go.

3. Press the seams toward the quilt center.

4. Once the border strips are sewn to the quilt, diagonally fold the quilt top with right sides together at one corner. Match your seams and pin in place through all the layers. Place a ruler along the folded edge of the quilt and draw a line through the last stitch in the seam and on through the border at a 45-degree angle.

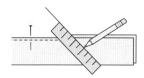

5. Align raw edges of the border strips and pin them in place along the drawn line.

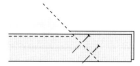

6. Stitch on the drawn line, being sure to start the line exactly at the spot where the border stitching finished. Do NOT stitch past the seam allowance.

7. Using your 45-degree marks on the ruler, make sure your miter is square. Trim a ¼" seam allowance and press open. Repeat for all four border corners. This completes your quilt top.

Sandwich the quilt top, back, and batting. Then quilt as desired.

TIP

I use 108" extra-wide backing fabric for my quilt backs because it eliminates the need for a seam. Plus, it's a great time saver. Why spend time piecing a quilt back when you could be starting your next quilt project!

CREATING THE BORDER SCALLOPS

1. The quilt should be quilted before you make your scallops. Then trace the scallop templates on freezer paper and cut on the traced line.

2. Using a chalk pencil, mark the scallops on all sides of the front of the quilt. Do NOT cut on the marked line as it is the sewing line.

BINDING THE QUILT

Since the border of this quilt is scalloped, you must use bias binding strips, which make it easy to follow the curves of the quilt.

1. Starting on the rounded part of the scallop, sew the tangerine print bias binding on the marked line, using a ¼" seam allowance and aligning the raw edges of the binding with the marked line (See page 11 for instructions on making bias binding).

2. Stitch to the base of the valley between the scallops. Stop with the needle down, pivot, then sew out of the valley. Be careful to avoid creating pleats.

3. Once the binding has been sewn in place, carefully cut away the excess border.

4. Turn the binding over to the back of the quilt and hand stitch it in place.

TIP

For all my hand quilting, I use Hobbs Heirloom 80/20 batting because it needles well and has no scrim. It also shrinks a tiny bit, creating that vintage look that I love.

In My Garden Bunny Block
18" finished

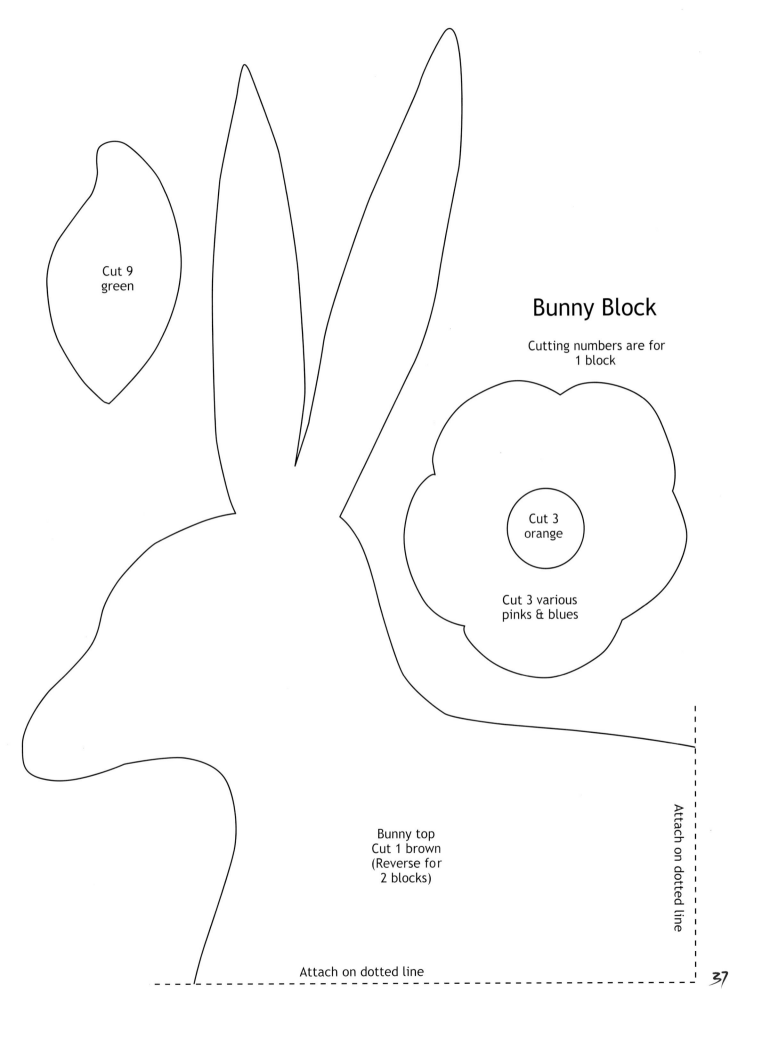

Cut 9
green

Bunny Block

Cutting numbers are for
1 block

Cut 3
orange

Cut 3 various
pinks & blues

Bunny top
Cut 1 brown
(Reverse for
2 blocks)

Attach on dotted line

Attach on dotted line

Bunny Block

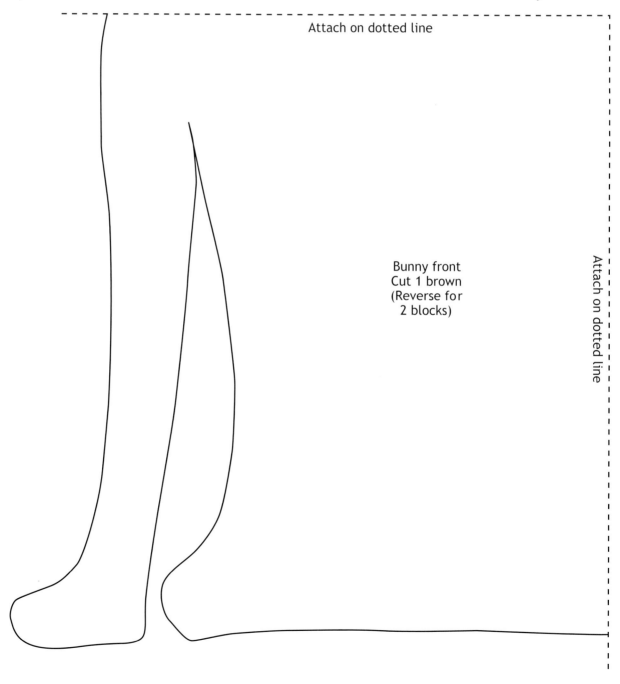

Attach on dotted line

Attach on dotted line

Bunny front
Cut 1 brown
(Reverse for
2 blocks)

38

Bunny Block

Bunny back
Cut 1 brown
(Reverse for
2 blocks)

In My Garden Bloom Block
18" finished

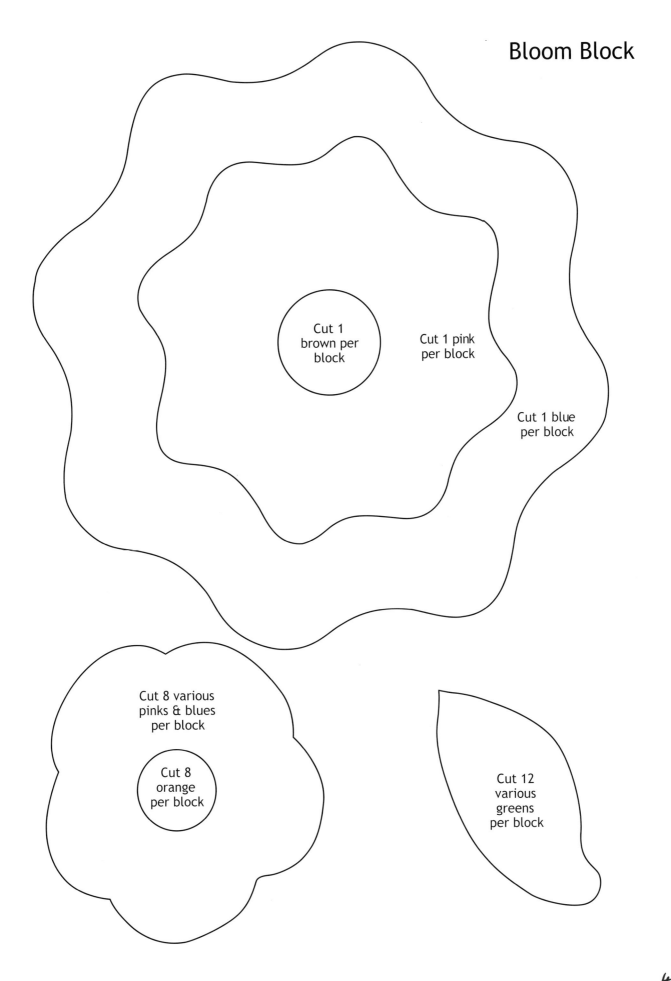

Bloom Block

Cut 1
brown per
block

Cut 1 pink
per block

Cut 1 blue
per block

Cut 8 various
pinks & blues
per block

Cut 8
orange
per block

Cut 12
various
greens
per block

41

In My Garden Carrot Block
18" finished

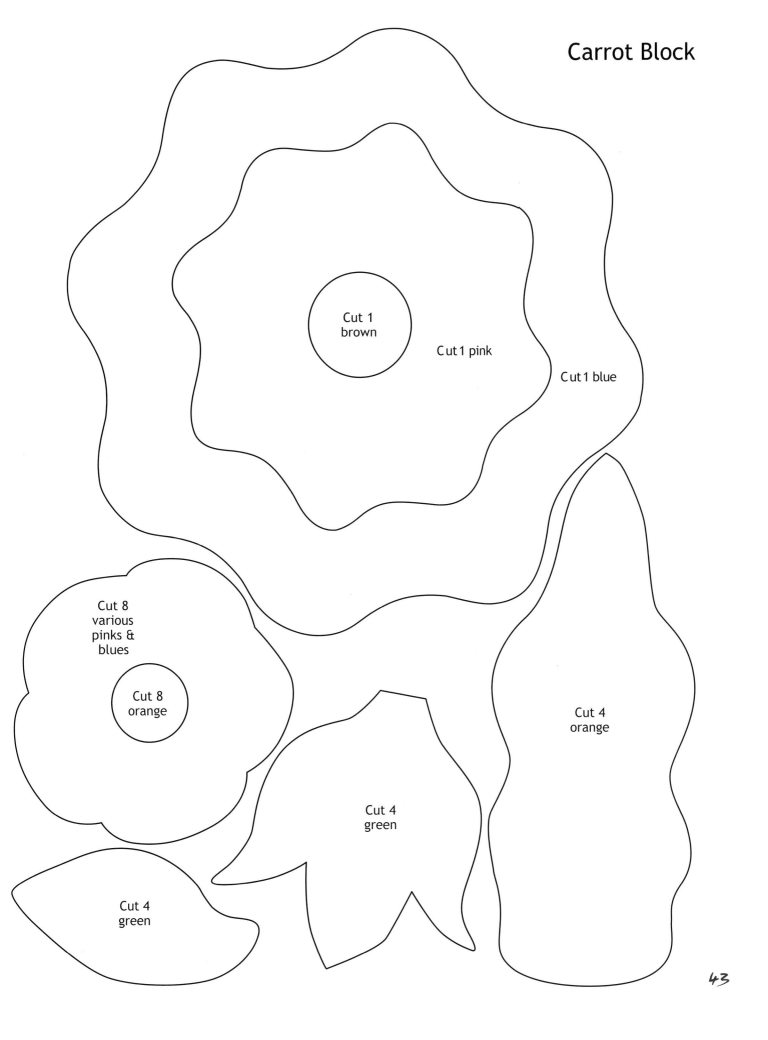

Carrot Block

Cut 1 brown

Cut 1 pink

Cut 1 blue

Cut 8 various pinks & blues

Cut 8 orange

Cut 4 orange

Cut 4 green

Cut 4 green

43

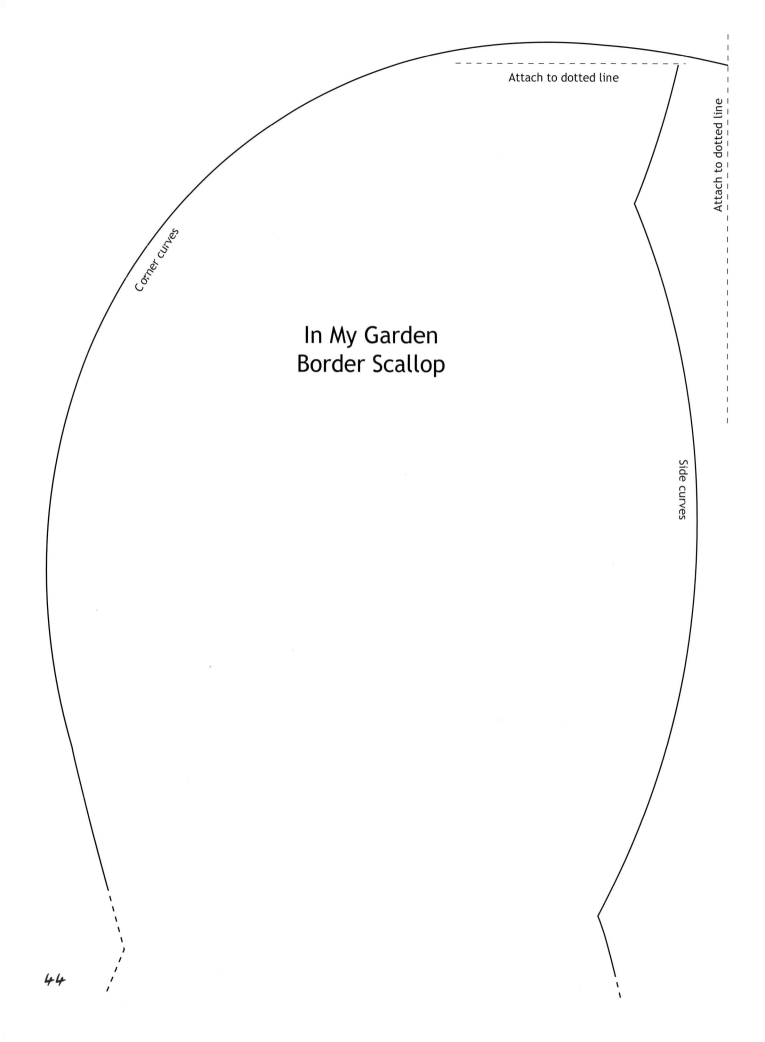

Attach to dotted line

Attach to dotted line

Corner curves

In My Garden
Border Scallop

Side curves

Finished size: 3.43" x 5.29"
Stitched by Dawn Heese

COTTAGE PINKEEP

A charming companion accent to the In My Garden quilt, this vintage-style pincushion is big enough to hold all your pins and needles. It is stitched with 2 strands of floss over 2 threads. The backstitches are stitched with 2 strands. In the lower right corner, I backstitched my grandmother's name as a remembrance to her with 1 strand of Weeks Dye Works Carrot (2226) embroidery floss. Personalize your pinkeep with a name that holds special meaning for you.

Material Requirements

- 28-count linen
- Weeks Dye Works embroidery floss: Sea Foam (1166), Peach Fuzz (1129), Carrot (2226), and Olive (2211)
- Crushed walnut shells (available at pet supply stores)

Finishing Instructions

1. Once you've completed your stitching, trim your stitched piece to 4 ¼" x 6 ¼".

2. Cut a 4 ¼" x 6 ¼" piece of muslin.

3. Baste the muslin to the back side of the stitched piece.

4. Cut a piece of 4 ½" x 6 ¼" ticking stripe fabric to back your pinkeep.

5. With right sides together and a ¼" seam allowance, sew the backing piece to the lined stitch piece. Leave a small opening to turn the pinkeep right side out.

6. Turn the pinkeep right side out, fill it with crushed walnut shells, and slip-stitch the opening closed.

TIP

Walnut shells work great as a pincushion filler because they give them weight and keep needles sharp. I purchase my walnut shells at Petco. They are marketed as bird or lizard litter and come in 7-pound bags, which seem to last forever.

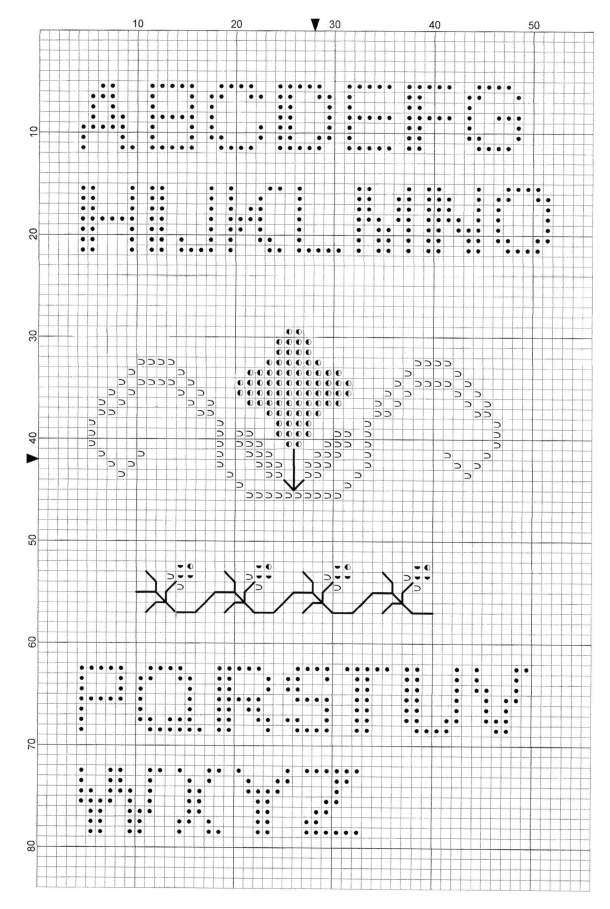

Legend:

- WDW-1166
- WDW-1129
- WDW-2226
- WDW-2211

Backstitches:

WDW-2211

48

GOSSAMER

Finished size: 80" x 80"
Finished block: 8"
Hand appliquéd and machine pieced by Dawn Heese
Machine quilted by Christy Gray/Katydid Design Studio

This quilt was inspired by one that I inherited from my great grandmother. The original was made of scraps on a sugar sack background. I love the fluttering movement of the butterflies. I made my winged beauties with a Moda fat quarter bundle, which gives the quilt visual variety while maintaining a consistent color palette. This project would make a great stash buster.

Fabric Requirements

Block backgrounds:
- 5 yards total of two different cream floral prints

Border:
- 1 ½ yards of one of the same cream floral prints used in the block backgrounds

Butterfly blocks:
- ½ yard brown print for butterfly bodies
- 12 fat quarters or equivalent yardage of various prints for butterfly wings

Backing:
- 2 ½ yards of 108"-wide backing fabric

Binding:
- 1 yard cream floral background print (I used one of the same background prints that I used in the block backgrounds)

Embroidery floss in a coordinating shade for butterfly antennae

Cutting Instructions

For butterfly blocks, cut:
- 81—8 ½" squares from cream floral print. Then apply Fray Check around the block edges.
- Appliqué templates on page 55.

For border, cut:
- 8—4 ½" strips the width of fabric from cream floral print. Then piece these strips together to create:
  - 2—4 ½" x 72 ½" strips and
  - 2—4 ½" x 80 ½" strips.
- Scallop template on page 56 from freezer paper.

For bias binding, see page 11.

Sewing Instructions

1. To ensure consistent placement of the appliqué shapes throughout the blocks, create an appliqué overlay from clear vinyl. Referring to your overlay for placement, appliqué shapes to the background fabric. Make 81 butterfly blocks.

2. Using two strands of embroidery floss, backstitch antennae on each butterfly (To create a backstitch, see stitch glossary on page 10). The backstitch I used is not perfect or precise because I wanted a more casual, primitive look.

3. At the end of each butterfly antennae, create a French knot, wrapping the thread around the needle 4 times (To create a French knot, see stitch glossary on page 10).

4. Referring to the assembly diagram on page 53, lay out all 81 butterfly blocks. **Note that the first row is flying up to the left, while the second row is flying down to the right. From there, the rows alternate.**

5. Sew 9 rows of 9 blocks each.

6. Sew together all 9 rows to create the quilt center.

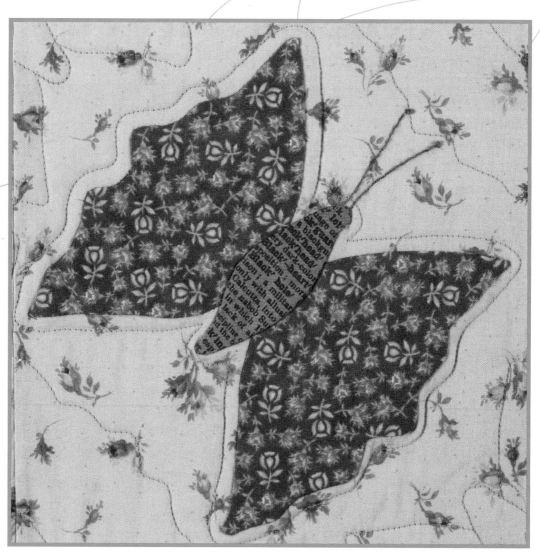

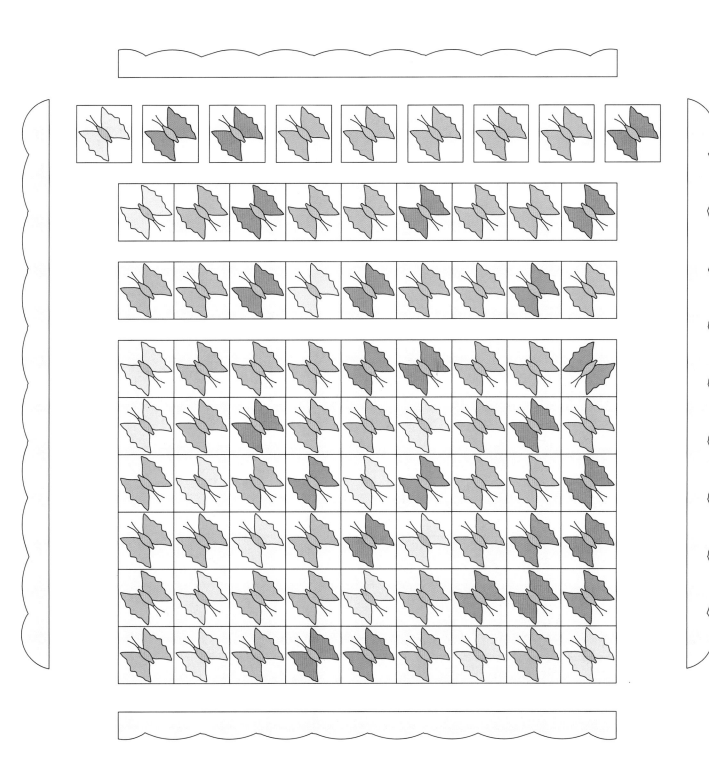

BORDER

1. Sew the 2—4 ½" x 72 ½" cream floral print strips to the top and bottom of the quilt center.

2. Sew the 2—4 ½" x 80 ½" cream floral print strips to the sides of the quilt center.

Finishing the Quilt

1. Sandwich the quilt top, batting, and backing. Then quilt as desired.

2. Trace the scallop template on page 56 on the quilt border (For more details on working with scallops, see page 35).

3. Sew the bias binding to the quilt (To create bias binding, see page 11).

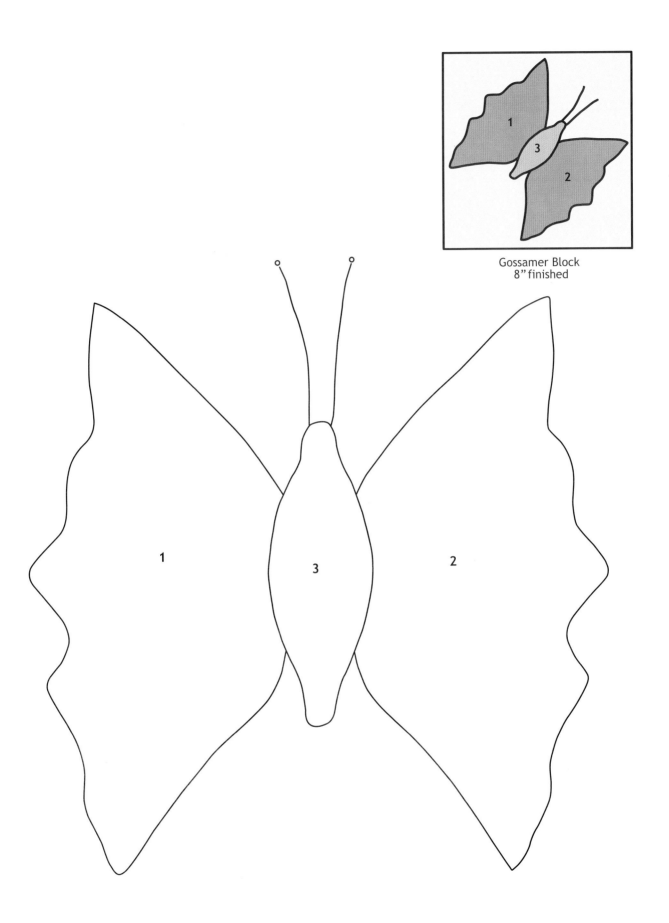

Gossamer Block
8" finished

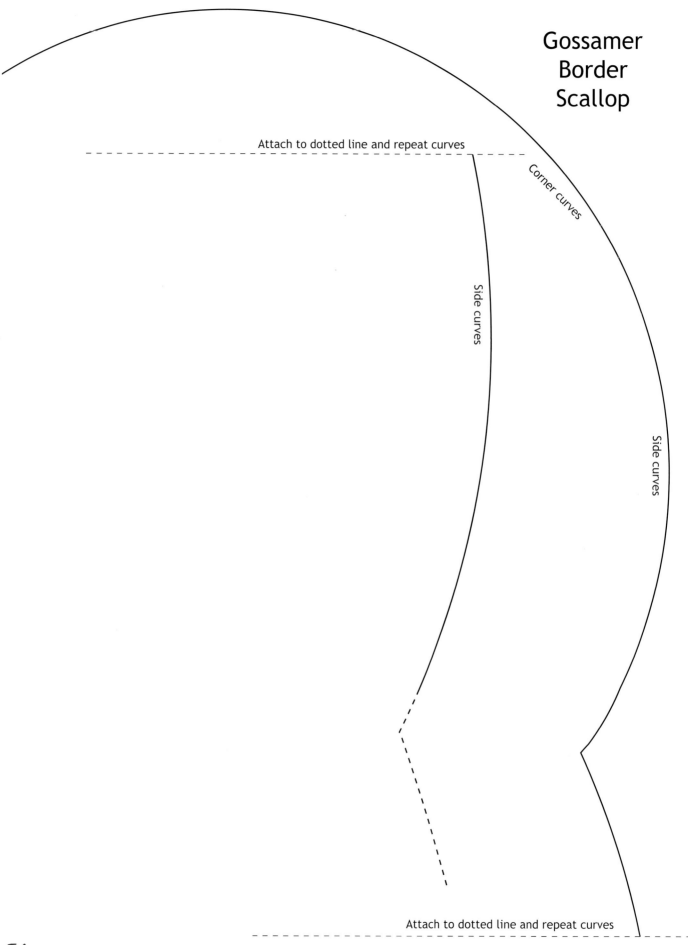

Gossamer
Border
Scallop

Attach to dotted line and repeat curves

Corner curves

Side curves

Side curves

Attach to dotted line and repeat curves

BUTTERFLY HOUSE SAMPLER

butterfly

abc house ghijk
def lmn
129
456 o
789
0. zyxwvuts rq p
1234567890 ·Aug.24,1913
ABCDEFGHIJKLMNOP.
·QRSTUVWXYZ.

Finished size: 7.79" x 9.07"
Stitched by Dawn Heese

Wildflowers bloom as butterflies flit amid the flowering beauty in this whimsical sampler. It is stitched with 2 strands over 2 threads. Backstitches are done with one strand and French knots are wrapped three times.

Material Requirements

- 28-count evenweave
- Frame with an 8" x 10" opening
- Weeks Dye Works embroidery floss: Stepping Stone (1289), Dolphin (1296), Basil (1291), Pebble (1151), Chablis (1139), Raspberry (1336), and Kudzu (2200)

Legend:

Symbol	Thread
●	WDW-1289
◐	WDW-1296
▼	WDW-1291
⊃	WDW-1151
◤	WDW-1139
▲	WDW-2200

Backstitches:

—————— WDW-2200

French knots:

◎ WDW-1336 wrapped 3x

 WDW-1296 (1 strand lazy daisy stitch for wings, backstitch for body)

Other Kansas City Star Quilts Books

Other Kansas City Star Quilts Books

PROJECT BOOKS:

Fan Quilt Memories by Jeanne Poore - 2000

Santa's Parade of Nursery Rhymes by Jeanne Poore - 2001

As the Crow Flies by Edie McGinnis - 2007

Sweet Inspirations by Pam Manning - 2007

Quilts Through the Camera's Eye
by Terry Clothier Thompson - 2007

Louisa May Alcott: Quilts of Her Life, Her Work, Her Heart by Terry Clothier Thompson - 2008

The Lincoln Museum Quilt: A Reproduction for Abe's Frontier Cabin by Barbara Brackman and Deb Rowden - 2008

Dinosaurs - Stomp, Chomp and Roar by Pam Manning - 2008

Carrie Hall's Sampler: Favorite Blocks from a Classic Pattern Collection by Barbara Brackman - 2008

Just Desserts: Quick Quilts Using Pre-cut Fabrics by Edie McGinnis - 2009

Christmas at Home: Quilts for Your Holiday Traditions by Christina DeArmond, Eula Lang and Kaye Spitzli - 2009

Geese in the Rose Garden by Dawn Heese - 2009

Winter Trees by Jane Kennedy - 2009

Ruby Red Dots: Fanciful Circle-Inspired Designs by Sheri M. Howard - 2009

Backyard Blooms by Barbara Jones - 2010

Not Your Grandmother's Quilt: An Applique Twist on Traditional Pieced Blocks by Sheri M. Howard - 2010

A Second Helping of Desserts: More Sweet Quilts Using Pre-cut Fabric by Edie McGinnis - 2010

HOT OFF THE PRESS PATTERNS:

Cabin in the Stars by Jan Patek - 2009

Arts & Crafts Sunflower by Barbara Brackman - 2009

Birthday Cake by Barbara Brackman - 2009

Strawberry Thief by Barbara Brackman - 2009

French Wrens by Dawn Heese - 2010

QUEEN BEES MYSTERIES:

Murders on Elderberry Road by Sally Goldenbaum - 2003

A Murder of Taste by Sally Goldenbaum - 2004

Murder on a Starry Night by Sally Goldenbaum - 2005

Dog-Gone Murder by Marnette Falley - 2008

DVD PROJECTS:

The Kansas City Stars: A Quilting Legacy - 2008